First World War
and Army of Occupation
War Diary
France, Belgium and Germany

58 DIVISION
174 Infantry Brigade
London Regiment
2/6 Battalion
2 September 1915 - 28 February 1916

WO95/3005/4

The Naval & Military Press Ltd
www.nmarchive.com
Published in association with The National Archives

Published by

The Naval & Military Press Ltd

Unit 10 Ridgewood Industrial Park,

Uckfield, East Sussex,

TN22 5QE England

Tel: +44 (0) 1825 749494

www.naval-military-press.com

www.nmarchive.com

This diary has been reprinted in facsimile from the original. Any imperfections are inevitably reproduced and the quality may fall short of modern type and cartographic standards.

© **Crown Copyright**
Images reproduced by permission of The National Archives, London, England, 2015.

Contents

Document type	Place/Title	Date From	Date To
Heading	WO95/3005/4		
Heading	War Diary of 2/6th Bn London Regt Vol 192		
War Diary	Ipswich	02/09/1915	19/09/1915
Miscellaneous	War Statement 2/6th Batt C.L.R Sep 1915		
War Diary	Ipswich	07/10/1915	26/10/1915
War Diary	Stowmarket	02/11/1915	02/11/1915
War Diary	Debenham	03/11/1915	03/11/1915
War Diary	Stradbroke	04/11/1915	04/11/1915
War Diary	Halesworth	05/11/1915	05/11/1915
War Diary	Wickham Market	06/11/1915	06/11/1915
War Diary	Stowmarket	11/11/1915	06/01/1916
War Diary	Sudbury	12/01/1916	28/02/1916

WO 95/3005/4

WAR DIARY
OF
2/6th Bn LONDON REGT

WAR DIARY
INTELLIGENCE SUMMARY

Army Form C. 2118.

Place	Date	Hour	Summary of Events and Information	Remarks and references to Appendices
IPSWICH.	2/9/15		2/Lt. M.A. MYER joined for duty date of gazette 31/7/15	RHC
	7/9/15	am 9.30	Bn. paraded for route march thisonae - Noston Heath returned 9.15. 8/9/15	RHC
	8/9/15		Linoned men of Bn. paraded and posted in accordance with Divisional scheme for Air Raids. No airships seen or heard. Returned to quarters 2.0 am Sept 9th	RHC
	9/9/15		Lionrel men of Bn. paraded and posted in accordance with Divisional scheme for Air Raids. No airships seen or heard. Returned to quarters 2.30 am Sept 10th	RHC
	11/9/15		Lionrel men of Bn. paraded and posted in accordance with Divisional Scheme for Air Raids. No airships seen or heard. Returned to quarters. 2.0. am Sept 12th	RHC
	15/9/15		Road piquets placed in accordance with Divisional scheme for Air Raids. Returned to quarters 4.0 am 16/9/15	RHC
	18/9/15	pm 5.20	Period of vigilance notified by Bde. H.Q.	RHC
	19/9/15	am 4.30	Orders received from Bde H.Q. to prepare to move and entrain 6.30 am. Bn. entrained for HALESWORTH and on arriving marched out and took up position from BLYFORD BRIDGE to 1st H of BLACKHEATH facing north. 8th Bn. on left no troops on right 3.0 pm concentrated marched to HALESWORTH entrained for IPSWICH 3.20 pm period of vigilance ended as notified by Bde H.Q.	RHC

Frank Allman Lt Col
Cmdg 2/5/15

War Statement
2/6th Batt C.L.R.

Sep 1915.

Organization

During the month of August 3 officers & a draft of 234 men have been sent to the 1st Battalion in France. This further call has again depleted the battalion which now only has trained men as specialists, the riflemen being all recruits. The battalion at the present moment is under strength owing to the difficulty experienced in obtaining drafts of recruits from the 3rd line. It would appear advantageous if as soon as a draft is sent to the Expeditionary force, a draft of recruits could be sent from the 3rd line immediately.

Training

All trained men are now being prepared as specialists. Recruit training is progressing favourably, but it would be advantageous if the N.C.O's who passed a special course of instruction in bayonet fighting & physical training at Aldershot could be transferred from the H.S. Batt. for training of recruits. It would also be advantageous if the trained men were permitted to fire another musketry course. Machine guns, range finders, & Compasses for NCOs are still urgently required.

Quarters & Subsistence

Quarters in billets at Ipswich remain satisfactory. During the month the battalion has been put on Central feeding with unusually satisfactory results.

Transport.

Extra wagons have been received but the Battalion is still short of Maltese carts. A field cooker has been received which will be useful in training companies in broiling.

Horses.

Draught mules have been received thus enabling all wagons on charge to be utilized. Extra chargers are still required.

Frank Collinson
Lt Col
Comdg 2/8th Batt CLR

Army Form C. 2118.

WAR DIARY
INTELLIGENCE SUMMARY.

(Erase heading not required.)

2/6 Bn. London Regt.

Instructions regarding War Diaries and Intelligence Summaries are contained in F.S. Regs., Part II. and the Staff Manual respectively. Title pages will be prepared in manuscript.

Place	Date	Hour	Summary of Events and Information	Remarks and references to Appendices
IPSWICH.	7/10/15.	a.m. 11.0.	Bn. paraded in Christchurch Park – Nominal Roll of munition workers prepared and submitted.	RMc
	9/10/15.		W.O. letters 30/9/15 and 5/10/15 received re reduction of strength to 600.	RMc.
	12/10/15.		Capt. S.T. Cooke seconded A/22/9/15 to act as R.T.O. –	RMc
			2/Lt Edwards granted 3 weeks sick leave –	RMc
	13/10/15.	p.m. 9.0.	Road picquets posted in accordance with Divisional Scheme for Air Raids. Zeppelins heard but not seen 11pm. Returned to quarters 6.0 am 14/10/15. –	RMc
	13/10/15.		Bde. orders received for Bn. move to Newmarket	RMc
	18/10/15.		Capt. Haines (billeting officer) and 4 NCO's proceeded to Newmarket on billeting duty	RMc
	22/10/15.	p.m. 12.15.	Undermentioned 2/Lt. to be Lieut. A/9/10/15. G.A.T. Smith, R. Loreday, E. Martin, R.J. Hartley, A.H. Test.	RMc
		a.m. 8.15.	1 N.C.O. and 163 men proceeded to 3/6 Bn. under Central force letter 10697(A) A/5/10/15. Lt. Smith, 2/Lt. Kendall and 5 NCO's conducting party.	RMc
		4 p.m.	Bn. paraded for Divisional Scheme. Occupied trenches at GREAT BEALINGS Returned to quarters	RMc

Frank Collman Lt. Col.
Comg 2/6 Bn CLR.

A.D.S.S./Forms/C. 2118.

Army Form C. 2118.

WAR DIARY

INTELLIGENCE SUMMARY

of 2/6 Bn. London Regt.

(Erase heading not required.)

Instructions regarding War Diaries and Intelligence Summaries are contained in F. S. Regs., Part II. and the Staff Manual respectively. Title pages will be prepared in manuscript.

Place	Date	Hour	Summary of Events and Information	Remarks and references to Appendices
IPSWICH.	23/10/15	10.0 am.	Conducting Party returned from 3/6 Bn. — — —	RMC.
	26/10/15	9.30 am.	Bn. paraded & marched out of IPSWICH for STOWMARKET.	
		3.15 pm.	Bn. arrived at STOWMARKET and accommodated in billets — — —	RMC.

Frank C Munoir? Lt.
Cmdg 2/6th Bn LR.

Army Form C.2118.

WAR DIARY
or
INTELLIGENCE SUMMARY
(Erase heading not required.)

2/6 Bn. London Regt.

Instructions regarding War Diaries and Intelligence Summaries are contained in F.S. Regs., Part II. and the Staff Manual respectively. Title pages will be prepared in manuscript.

Place	Date	Hour	Summary of Events and Information	Remarks and references to Appendices
STOWMARKET	2/11/15	8.45 am	17 Officers, 1 med. Officer (attached) and 450 other ranks paraded for Brigade took with transport. Marched to DEBENHAM with field operations en route - Scheme 2/6 Bn. acting as hostile force delaying remainder of Brigade entering DEBENHAM - Close billeted. Remainder of 2/6 B. left at STOWMARKET under Capt. Tillard. CAPT. TILLARD	RMG RMG
DEBENHAM	3/11/15		Marched to STRADBROKE and took up defensive position covering village west of the church facing north. 2/8 Bn. on right - east of church. Practised feeding men in their defensive position - Close billeted at STRADBROKE	RMG
STRADBROKE	4/11/15		Marched to HALESWORTH with field operations in HEVENINGHAM PARK - Scheme 2/5 Bn. and 2/6 Bn. less 2 Coys hostile force delaying advance of 2/6 & 1/8 Bns - 2 Coys 2/7 Bn. escort to transport - Close billeted at HALESWORTH	RMG
HALESWORTH	5/11/15		Marched in Brigade to WICKHAM MARKET - Close billeted at WICKHAM MARKET	RMG
WICKHAM MARKET	6/11/15		Marched to STOWMARKET and took up previous billets relinquished on 2/11/15 medical inspection en route.	RMG
STOWMARKET	11/11/15		Maj. F.G. TUCKER returned to Bn duty from 58th Divl. Staff (attached)	RMG
	16/11/15	7.45 am	Bn paraded for Bde operations Scheme 2/6 Bn defending STOWMARKET across 2/5 7/+ 2/8 Bns. Posted. Thrown up near BAYLHAM to surprise enemys advance either light rearguard action towards NEEDHAM MARKET until reinforced at 4pm. Returned to quarters 4.45pm	RMG

1577 Wt.W10791/1773 500,000 1/15 D.D.& S.S./Forms/C. 2118.

Army Form C. 2118.

WAR DIARY
or
INTELLIGENCE SUMMARY
(Erase heading not required.)

2/13 Bn London Regt

Place	Date	Hour	Summary of Events and Information	Remarks and references to Appendices
STOWMARKET	30/11/15	a.m. 9.0	Bn. paraded for Bde operations. Scheme simultaneous attack on flag position at WILLISHAM from 3 points 2/6 Bn from north 2/7 from East 2/8 from South. 2/13 Bn intercepting enemys line of retreat westward. Returned to quarters 4.40 pm.	RMC
	25/11/15		2/Lts H.W. POTTS L.J.S. HILL K.R.G. DICKINSON proceeded to 3/6 Bn in accordance with Central force order M.A MYER I. MACFARLANE 1387 d/13/9/15 reducing establishment 8 Officers.	

Frank Collinson Lt Col.
Comdg. 2/6 Bn London Regt

Army Form C. 2118.

WAR DIARY
or
INTELLIGENCE SUMMARY.

(Erase heading not required.)

2/6th Bn. London Regt.

Instructions regarding War Diaries and Intelligence Summaries are contained in F. S. Regs., Part II. and the Staff Manual respectively. Title pages will be prepared in manuscript.

Place	Date	Hour	Summary of Events and Information	Remarks and references to Appendices
STOWMARKET	1/12/15		40 men transferred to 3/6 Bn to reduce establishment to 600	RWC
	3/12/15		19 men transferred to 101st Provisional Battalion (under age)	RWC
	16/12/15		Lieut. G.A.T. SMITH proceeded to 101st Provisional Battalion (fit for Home Service only)	RWC
	27/12/15 30/12/15 6/12/15		No 4 musketry party at Bardsey	RWC

Frank Colluan
Lieut. Colonel,
comdg. 2/6th. Bn. City of London Rifles.

Army Form C. 2118.

WAR DIARY
or
INTELLIGENCE SUMMARY.
(Erase heading not required.)

2/6 Bn. London Regt.

Instructions regarding War Diaries and Intelligence Summaries are contained in F.S. Regs., Part II. and the Staff Manual respectively. Title pages will be prepared in manuscript.

Place	Date	Hour	Summary of Events and Information	Remarks and references to Appendices
STOWMARKET	6/1/16	9.0 am	Bn. paraded and marched out of STOWMARKET for SUDBURY.	RMC
SUDBURY		4.15 pm	Bn. arrived at SUDBURY and accommodated in billets	RMC
	12/1/16		5 officers from 3/6 Bn. reported for duty and taken on strength	RMC
"	21/1/16		First batch of "Derby" recruits arrived	RMC
"	28/1/16	8.0 pm	Bn. paraded and emergency guard detailed for possible air raid on warning from Brigade H.Q. Dismissed at 12 midnight	RMC

R H Collins
Capt & adjt.

[Stamp: 56th (LONDON) DIVISION 3 FEB 1916 GENERAL STAFF]

Page 1

Army Form C. 2118.

2/6 Bn. London Regt

WAR DIARY
or
INTELLIGENCE SUMMARY
(Erase heading not required.)

Place	Date	Hour	Summary of Events and Information	Remarks and references to Appendices
SUDBURY	1/2/16		21 Recruits arrived from Adm. Centre	R.A.C
	2/2/16		8 " " " "	R.A.C
	3/2/16		23 " " " "	R.A.C
	4/2/16		9 " " " "	R.A.C
	5/2/16		Inspection of Bn. by Major-General Dickson - Inspector of Infantry.	DICKSON. R.A.C R.A.C.
	9/2/16		28 Recruits arrived from Adm. Centre	R.A.C.
	10/2/16		11 " " " "	R.A.C
	11/2/16		5 " " " " Inspection of Recruits by G.O.C. 174th Inf. Bde.	R.A.C
	12/2/16		6. Recruits arrived from Adm. Centre	R.A.C.

Page 2. Army Form C. 2118.

WAR DIARY
or
INTELLIGENCE SUMMARY.

2/6 Bn. London Regt.

(Erase heading not required.)

Place	Date	Hour	Summary of Events and Information	Remarks and references to Appendices
SUDBURY	14/2/16		9 Recruits arrived from Adm. Centre.	RHG
"	21/2/16		Inspection of Battalion by G.O.C. 58th (London) Division	RHG
"	28/2/16		Inspection of Recruits and Regimental Employ and Instructional Staff by G.O.C. 174th Infantry Bde.	RHG

R H Collins
Capt & Adjt
2/6 Bn. London Regt

www.ingramcontent.com/pod-product-compliance
Lightning Source LLC
Chambersburg PA
CBHW081514160426

43193CB00014B/2685